My Life of High Adventure

My Life of High Adventure

Leonard Restall, PhD

To order additional copies of this book, contact:
Xlibris
NZ TFN: 0800 008 756 (Toll Free inside the NZ)
NZ Local: 9-801 1905 (+64 9801 1905 from outside New Zealand)
www.Xlibris.co.nz
Orders@Xlibris.co.nz
810230

CONTENTS

CHAPTER 1

My Life of High Adventure

Very rarely would a life of high adventure start on the mountain top but the opportunities in life could cause one to aspire mountain top experiences. This is what has happened to me during my 91 years so far. It can be, and I hope that it will inspire you to find out just how these things can come about without any serendipitous circumstance being planned for. Not that planning is not essential to gain higher rewards.

I was born at Caxton Rd, Wood Green in London on 14 March 1929 during the Great Depression and lived with my parents at this address for a short time, as I had been informed, before moving into my Grandparents large Georgian House at 79 Crayford Rd, Holloway, London. It would have been for a short time before moving to a large council estate in Barking, Dagenham about 1934. (This house is still standing and is counted as a historic building. There had been a move to demolish it and build a supermarket complex on the site but with so many protests against such a move, it still remains.)

This estate was one of the biggest ones in England at that time and was built to accommodate workers for the Ford Motor Company in Dagenham. Our house was a new brick-built double-storey building with all the modern appliances for that day. It had a front garden and also a large back garden for growing vegetables. It was a very comfortable home, near to schools and shops and good bus services.

My Grandparents had been business people in South Wales during the great depression in which they lost most of their possessions and eventually moved to London. Their house was a large Georgian three-storey one with a basement; it provided enough room for us and my uncle Aaron and Auntie Anne. Grandfather worked as a security man for a jeweller in Regents St and one time took me to show me around all the valuable silverware and also showed me a pistol that he carried during night work. He was glad that he never had to use the pistol.

Grandad liked walking much and often took me for long walks to Highgate, Hampstead Heath and also to Regents Park Zoo. Both Grandparents went to Chapel on a Sunday, which had been their custom in Wales. Grandad took me to see the procession of the Coronation of King George VI. He had me standing on his shoulders in Regents St as the Gold coach and the remainder of the procession passed by. It was an unforgettable experience. I had a great liking for Grandad. He was kind and helped me a lot in my early life.

My father was an electrical engineer for the London Transport Passenger Board that runs the underground rail system This was the only job that I can remember him having before he eventually retired. He had been responsible for fitting the very first escalator system into the underground, I think it was at either Leicester Square or Piccadilly Circus.

He was an avid radio buff but also an excellent gardener winning many prizes for his front garden display for many years. His roses and begonias were a speciality and delighted many visitors to view his garden. I can still remember vividly the runner beans that he grew each year. They were 'as long as your arm' is what he used to say about them. This trait for good gardening seemed to be passed on to my older brother, Norman, who won many prizes at shows for his produce. But it never caught on for me other than for growing good roses which became my beloved Rita's favourite flower.

Dad, served in the Royal Engineers in World War 1 and was used to established searchlight installations, one being on the Eddystone lighthouse near Plymouth.

He was based on the island of St Helena for a period during that war. He never spoke much about the war or his military service. This seemed to be a feature of these who took part in the World War 1.

Dad had much influence on me. He was a very smart man and maintained impeccable neatness going to and from work. His shoes were always highly polished and he always wore a clean white starched collar. I suppose it was his military side showing out. He was a very good golfer and he often took me out to play and gave me the desire to play sport, which carried on later in my life. Dad was also a very good writer or penmanship. He used to write in old English script even when he filled in his coupons for the football pools, a weekly game of chance. He told me that he was once accepted for membership to a golf club, not on his playing ability, but by the illuminated address he submitted for his application. This is something that has stuck with me.

I used to encourage my students at school to also watch their writing especially when applying for a job, and preferably use a pen and ink rather than a biro pen.

Another strong influence was his love for classical singing and music, such as Caruso and opera. He took me to see Othello and Tosca in a London theatre and also to a concert given by the Philadelphia Orchestra conducted by Eugene Ormandy at the Harringay Arena. We went to many soccer games, either at the Tottenham ground or Arsenal and also to two FA cup finals. He also took me several times to dog racing and speedway racing. I was developing a strong attitude towards sports and physical fitness which was to later become a major part of my life, which I am thankful for.

I was privileged to have been able to pray for him whilst he was in hospital. He was not religious but may have counted himself as one for England was a Christian country. He did sometimes come to a church with us when he came to stay with us in Plymouth. This would have been in his latter years of his life. Unfortunately I was in England when both he and my Mother died.

My mother's influence on me was through her general industrious ways and attention to neatness in dress and deportment. I won a school prize for having the best-kept shoes in the school for the year, but it was my mother who did the cleaning of them much to my shame. She was a perfect cook and had served some of her younger life in 'service' that is serving someone else. Both parents loved me unreservedly, as well as for my three brothers and sister and never showed any dislike to my often rebellious behaviour, and through the difficult times during the war. How they coped is a mystery in itself. She was heart broken when an older brother off mine, Alec, was killed having been knocked down by a motor cyclist. In those days our only playing grounds were outside in the street. There was usually not many vehicles driving along our road so it was safe. It was the tragic end for a brilliant student who had a promising future snuffed out by an accident. The person who did it was not at fault and also was very upset by the genuine accident.

My schooling or lack of it was largely disrupted because of the War starting in 1939. Up to that time, I attended Dorothy Barley School, which was in the next road to where I was living. At the time I started, the school had only just been built and was quite modern when compared to many of the schools in England. It had two sections: an Infants section for children starting at the age of 5 years and a Junior section terminating at the age of 11 years.

The emphasis during the Infants section was on reading and numeracy together with neatness in writing with pen and ink from wells in each desktop. They were using a style that came to be known as the 'Barking' style of writing. Care in writing has remained with me now more than 80 years on. I could read well and be keen on sports.

By the time I was in the Junior school the war was imminent and had started soon after. Plans to evacuate the whole school to other parts of England were soon put into operation and I was got ready quickly by my mother to leave by train for a small town or village, Langport East in Somerset. This was quite a strange experience for a Londoner to be now living in the unusual position of the country life.

I was first billeted with a farm couple who had some cows for milk but mainly grew cider apples. Daily life became that of a farmer getting up early in the morning to go with the couple milking by hand the small number of cows they had. This and many other of the tasks required on the farm such as haymaking and thrashing of the wheat became a part of my routine.

I did not stay long in Langport as an evacuees because at that time there had not been any air raids over London so my Mother brought me back to Barking in early 1940.

Schools lessons were taken in a church hall and mainly consisted of music, singing and storytelling. One teacher, Mr Evans, a Welsh man, led us in singing many of the well known Welsh songs with great gusto. Mr Evans became one of my favourite teachers but I did not stay with him long enough to make much impression on my learning. So any chance of passing the 11 plus exam, which was the exam required to enter either Grammar School or Secondary School was beyond me, so I thought.

My next school was an elementary school, this was before comprehensive schools were established. It was for children aged 11 years to 14 years. But at this time air raids were a regular occurrence with German aircraft flying directly over our area on their way to London. They would use the River Thames as a guide. Many times bombs were dropped well before the aircraft got to London so they could then scarper for home.

The Battle of Britain occurred during this time in September 1940. This was where the RAF attempted to intercept the German bombers as they started to travel towards London. We had an aerodrome at Hornchurch, not too far from home where there were spitfires and hurricane fighters based. It was at this aerodrome that I met with Jean Batten the famous aviator from New Zealand that had flown single-handed around the world. I got her autograph that day in 1936. I was also to meet her in Blenheim, New Zealand in 1962 and told her that I had met her at Hornchurch. She said that she enjoyed the place immensely and was treated so well there in the Officers Mess. Unfortunately, I lost her autograph as time went on.

There were regular 'dog fights' overhead and several enemy aircraft were shot down in our area. We had some close calls to our home and the school was bombed with an incendiary container of incendiary bombs, a thousand in all, but most landed on the sports field. Several landed on the school hall and burnt it out.

Most of my school days in an air raid shelter, which was a cloakroom protected with sandbags. Very little school subjects were done during the times in the shelter. Some of my time, whenever there was no air raid, would be in the woodwork section learning carpentry. I quite liked this and could picture myself working at this when I had left school.

The terror of V1(doodlebug) and V2 (rocket missile) start to terrorise London. We had a V1 drop about 400 meters from my home and I experienced a V2 at close quarters when leaving the Bank of England in the City. It landed on a police station in one of the adjacent streets to the Bank and flattened the tall building completely leaving a very deep crater as a result.

This type of bomb was very frightening for there was no warning with it, it just came out of the sky from a very high altitude. If this had carried on for very much longer I think there could have been a capitulation. Fortunately, this type of bombing did not continue for too long as the sites where these may have come from were heavily bombed by the allies.

Family photo Len & Rita in centre

At home, we had our own underground Anderson shelter made out of corrugated iron and sunk below ground level. It was our usual practice at home to move down into it at night as soon as the alarms were given and stay there for the night. They gave some measure of security but would not stand up to a direct or near-direct hit. One of my classmates and his whole family were killed when their shelter received a direct hit and it blew the shelter up on to a two-storied house about 100 metres away.

Air raids we're a regular horror and left us wondering whether we would come through it safely. They upset our night and day routines. The siren would go early in the evening and we would not get the all-clear until the morning. So as soon as the siren would sound indicating an air raid, then Mother would have us take our pyjamas with us down to the shelter for the night. We were quite comfortable in the shelter with electric lights but not much else.

These raids were very frightening with enemy

aircraft coming just after the air raid sirens had sounded. The heavy drone of the Dornier and Junker bombers being met with heavy anti-aircraft guns firing was very noisy and then would come the 'whistle' of bombs being dropped. One wondered where they were falling but those which dropped close to our home were enormous explosions that scared us. This would go on for several hours. The aircraft that made their way to London would now be met on the way back with more shelling by the anti-aircraft guns. It seemed to go on relentless for hours. The closest bomb to land near us was a V1 flying bomb which landed about 400 metres from us. The first land mine to be dropped was in the road next to our road.

I had given my Father a hand in digging the deep hole to put the Anderson shelter in. There was only a small part of the top showing out of the ground, so we felt safe other than for a direct hit. The shelters were made out of heavy corrugated iron and were issued free by the local councils. We used to sometimes get four of us in the shelter for the night.

During these years I did not sense it as being one of adventure but rather of survival. I do recall having a personal sense of achievement motivation although would not have identified as such then as a child. Nevertheless it was a part of my individuality that I came to recognise in later life. I always wanted to win and not lose, to be at the top of the class rather than lower down the order, and was always looking towards success and disappointed if I was not successful. This particular trait became more prominent as I grew older.

All this was going on when it was time for me to leave school at the age of 14 years to go to work. We did not get much preparation from school for work other than experience for me doing some woodwork without machine tools. I did not at that time think that I was too young to be leaving school to go to work because that was what most children were doing What a difference it is today with guidance counsellors and others preparing student for the work force. But did it make a difference to me? No. We were forced to mature possibly ahead of time.

CHAPTER 2

My First Jobs

The thought of leaving school to get a job and earn some money was very appealing for me, but what sort of work should I have been aiming for? At that time I had never received any counselling or given any advice except from parents as to what type of job should I go for. The options of choice were not for me. Sure I preferred woodworking because I was quite good at it and this may have been on my mind for quite a bit.

Whatever job I got I wanted to do well at it and woodworking in the form of cabinet making would fill that bill for me. But that option did not present itself to me, but it never left my mind. Was it the fact that I could do it well and so would get more recognition and satisfaction from it.

Later I was to learn that there are many people in jobs which they are not suitable for, and this can be as high as 80%. A knowledge of these things would have helped me much. I still had the desire to excel at whatever

I did and therefore, my achievement motivation was high. But I didn't recognise it as such. I suppose I was unknowingly seeking after high adventure in the work that I would be doing.

In those days the leaving age from school was 14 years unless one went to Grammar School, which was never my option so my mind was set on finding work. Maybe the thought of earning money would have provided some immediate motivation, but was unlikely to last. Today young people have the opportunity of finding out the jobs that they would have a high level of success at depending on their individuality. so to aim at a high level of achievement as well as adventure is within the grasp of everyone.

I left school at the age of 14 while the war was still on to get a job. The first job I took to earn some money was gained for me by my father who worked in the City. He got me a job with an Advertising Agency and publications distributor, called Leathwaite and Simmons in Gracechurch Street, not far from the Bank of England. It was a good experience but not one that I wanted to work at for long. I was to deliver books and publications to many firms in the London City area It kept me fit for playing football.

But woodwork was still in my mind to work at. An opportunity came up to work for a cabinet-making firm, Beresford and Hicks in Hoxton, near Shoreditch. This firm was a highly reputed firm doing work for the Buckingham Palace and for other members of the royal family such as the Duke of Gloucester. This firm was also involved during the war in making parts for the 'Mosquito' aircraft, which were mainly wood, laminated spruce, with a metal outer skin.

This job gave me good experience working with other skilled cabinet makers, but it was about 10 miles from home. This meant much travelling by cycle and in all kinds of bad weather such as fog, snow, rain, and also the occasional air raid. I used to leave home at 6.30 am to be at work by 7.30 am and then work until 5 pm. I eventually got another job in Ilford working for a very good furniture store, Harrison and Gibsons which made and repaired quality furniture, but this was not to last too long before I was attracted to join the RAF in 1946. How this began was an adventure unfolding after a football game I had played in. This was to make a remarkable change to my future.

My Birthplace - home Wood
Green North London 1929

CHAPTER 3

The Start of My Adventure

How this came about

My story starts as a young man of seventeen workings as a cabinet maker but very interested in sport, particularly soccer. I eventually played for a London club, Leyton, and during a game against a Tottenham Hotspur team I was able to meet with Ted Ditchburn, the then-current England goalkeeper, Ted was also a PTI in the RAF. After talking with Ted, he suggested, persuasively, for me to become a PTI in the RAF. I took up the challenge and applied at a recruiting office and was accepted for training. I really didn't know what I would be letting myself in for but it was worth the challenge.

My first training, 'square bashing' was done at Bridgnorth, near Wolverhampton and then I was moved to Cardington in Bedford to undergo an NCO's course. This was my preparation in eventually becoming a corporal. After six weeks of training, I was then moved to the School of PT in Cosford, just outside Wolverhampton to commence basic training as u/t PTI.

This was a period of training in which we had to be smart and well-disciplined in marching and moving as a group. This same attitude had to be exercised in the barrack rooms as well. The fact that we would soon be promoted to corporal had the effect of making us aware more about being smart and being well turned out.

Our barrack room had twenty-bed spaces with double-tiered beds. Beds had to be made up daily and some of our uniforms had to be carefully folded and stacked on a shelf close to our bed space. If it did not conform to the standard. required by the inspecting officer or NCO it was pulled off the shelf and had to be folded again.

These barrack rooms were very cold in winter and only had a potbelly stove to warm the room. This was barely sufficient. I can remember ice melting on the roof of the barrack block, leaking on to the floor of the room and then freezing inside the barrack room. My adventure had surely begun!

Air Force Days RAF - School of P T staff photo

The PTI training was very challenging as I had left school at the age of 14 without any educational qualification, but I was prepared to accept the new challenge with a 'second chance'. This attitude was to become a strong point in my favour for future success. During this period of training, the School was involved with training for a display team for the Royal Tournament to be held in London at Olympia. I was included in this display team, with 150 others.

The display consisted of various formations of the men performing calisthenic type of exercises together with maze running to the music being played by the Central Band of the RAF. with the 150 men performing it would have been quite spectacular. I enjoyed it much and can still perform some of the exercise from memory. It was estimated that we ran about one mile during the maze running.

It was a thrilling time performing twice a day for 10 days and during one performance seen by the King and Queen and the two Princesses. (King George VI; Princess Elizabeth and Margaret). We also performed at several other places in England: Blackpool, Chiswick and Birmingham. I was chosen to be on the red carpet as a guard of honour for when the Royal party arrived.

My course instructor was a Sergeant Black and the Officer i/c was Flt.Lt MacDonald. After training, I was made a corporal and for some good reason, known to the powers to be, retained to become a staff instructor at the school. I gained a good result from my initial course so this may be the reason why I was selected to become a staff instructor. I had taken several initial courses and also completed an advanced course with top marks, so I now was made a senior instructor taking the advanced courses.

The very first Advanced PTI Course RNZAF 1956

Two well known RAF PTI's were on that first course:

W/O Aldridge, from 'Red Beret; fame and a W/O Worder, known as 'chang' who had served with Lawrence of Arabia This was quite an awesome task to be taking senior instructors with far more experience than I would possibly ever have, but I survived.

I was promoted to Sergeant and a major event in my life occurred when I was attached to a School of Training Organisation and Management course at Cosford. I passed this course with an A+, but one thing that has made an enormous difference to me is the realisation that motivation is a major factor in success. This became a key to my further success and was in line with my achievement motivation. Yet I had not fully understood what was needed to release this motivation towards anything specifically. But that was to come. Motivation needs to be focussed on something tangible and understood. This was growing in me at a fast rate.

This would be a driving force for me in years to come. But at that time, I had two strong 'desires' or dreams: one was to become a doctor or a teacher, but I did not have the necessary education to pursue either those careers unless……. I started to gain educational qualification by eventually gaining matriculation which enabled me to go to a Training College or University. More on this later.

I played rugby for Cosford and basketball, also fencing, and ended at the Royal Tournament for five years with gaining runner up for the Bayonet competition. I became RAF champion in 1950 and represented the RAF in Inter-Service completion. Fencing became one of my strong passions after having done a course with a French Professor, Boutie Raimond.

I was to become the main fencing instructor on the

school, yet not having even seen a foil, epee or sabre before in my life other than in films with Errol Flynn This looked like a rerun of hollywood for me. But the personal challenge was within me to excel at this sport, which I did. I was close to selection for the 1950 Empire Games in New Zealand, but missed out to a person that I had beaten at epee, but he beat me at foil and sabre.

I suppose I must have been getting disillusioned by being on the staff since having passed my course, and without any postings to faraway places that the possibility of transferring to another country Air Force like Australia, Canada or New Zealand entered my thinking. It was rather like imaging what this far away country would be like. I had only read about its rugby prowess and it was because I was playing rugby, New Zealand the epitome of rugby, became my choice to go to. I was accepted on 17th August 1952. No turning back now! The Adventure was now proceeding at a fast rate.

Various questions would continually be coming up in my mind such as,' What is the country like? and what will my position be? But like all adventures, the story is not told until it is finished.

My Journey to New Zealand

With much excitement the 18th August 1952 had come for me to start on another part of my adventure: going on my own to a country I had no knowledge of other than its rugby tradition, and not knowing anyone in that country, So there was some apprehension as well as the excitement.

I travelled by train, leaving from Kings Cross station to Glasgow. I was farewelled by my Dad and brother Norman. We had a couple of drinks together and some photographs together visited my Grandmother and Auntie in Holloway and said farewell until we meet again, not quite knowing when that would be. I loved my Dad and brothers and sister and was quite close to them. The farewell was not very much a problem for me because having been in the RAF I was often away from home, and this occasion did not seem to be much different. But I had never been out of England.

The train journey was a long one and the first time that I had been to Scotland. There was a sense of excitement when I met up with some other of the RAF draft that also was going to NewZealand.so we became good friends for the journey. We embarked on the TSS Captain Cook on the 18th August in readiness for sailing on the 19th.

TSS Captain Cook August 1952

On the evening of the 18th August while walking on the main deck with a friend a steward came along with plates of sandwiches before the evening meal. Two young very attractive girls spotted us with the sandwiches and wanted to know where we got them from. I said "a steward had just brought them out" They were about to hurry off to find the steward so I said, "you can have these and I will go and get some more". I gave up my plate to these two girls, Rita Morris and Margaret Sanders.

Margaret Sanders, a friend of Rita's on Captain Cook

This was the start of a strong friendship for the remainder of the six weeks journey to New Zealand. Both Rita and Margaret were travelling to New Zealand to work for the then General Post Office as telephone operators. This was their job in Nottingham before deciding to go to New Zealand. They were very good friends for each other and had been for years.

Every day doing the voyage from early morning to 11 pm I spent with Rita, sunbathing, sharing our backgrounds, having the occasional drink together, and attending entertainment events such as films and dances. It was a wonderful time with perfect summer weather and it seemed like a holiday of a lifetime. We had a couple of stops on the way, at Curacao and Bilboa in the Panama canal area. It was becoming like a courtship for we knew each other so well, with our likes and dislikes. But it was soon to come to an end on the 24th September.1952 when we arrived in Wellington harbour in the late afternoon and were to remain on the ship until disembarking on the 25th.

Rita and Margaret were to stay in Wellington in the Post Office Hostel and I was to travel further south to Christchurch to the RNZAF base at Wigram. We said our farewells sadly and thought that was the end of a wonderful friendship and that was the end of it. I suppose both of us had boy or girlfriends before but not so long continuously together.

Rita phoned me daily at Wigram, usually early in the morning before I started my training. This went on for several weeks and during that phase of our lives Rita would travel down from Wellington or I would travel to Wellington for weekends together. It was during one of these weekends that we decided to get married, an adventure that we had not tried before. We were obviously in love with each other for we could not stand being away from each other. A challenge coming with this adventure was that we knew very few people, had limited financial backing other than the salary we were getting to get married, but we loved each other and that had a calming effect upon the challenge.

Wife Rita - Our first home in NZ December 1952

We were married on 22nd December 1952 at the Hereford Street Registry Office. Our first home was in St Elmo's Court also in Hereford Street so it was very convenient for us. We only had two witnesses, at the wedding because we had only just come into the country. One of the witnesses was a work colleague of mine and his wife. All this was to happen over a plate of sandwiches. I wonder what was in those sandwiches?

CHAPTER 4

The RNZAF Career

My job in the RNZAF started on 18th September 1952 and my first posting was to the Base at Wigram in Christchurch, NZ. This was a large training Base for various trades as well as for aircrew. I think it was the main one for training pilots and navigators. So it looked from the start that I would be very busy in the fitness line. I was young enough at the age of 23 and very fit to look forward to an enjoyable and beneficial time there, although when I first arrived in 1952 having come from a huge Base in England I was rather apprehensive as to what to expect. But adventure can start from any position or condition and this was an adventure. So my attitude must be in agreement with my desire to become an adventurer.

On arriving at the Base we were kitted out, given a dormitory to be my home for the next weeks or so and the process of indoctrination or initiation of the Air Force requirements needed to be absorbed in readiness for the tasks ahead. We had to become familiar with the RNZAF regulations and procedures and the fact that shops in the local town and city were closed from Friday evening until the Monday.

This initiation course took several weeks and then I was moved to the PT Section to begin my work of fitness for trainees on the Base. I found the new facilities rather sparse as compared to the RAF School of PT with its large gymnasium and swimming pool. Now I would be performing in a wooden building that had been a hangar for the 'Southern Cross' aeroplane.

But I soon got to make the adjustments to my new country and job with enthusiasm.

This Base became the training school for future PTIs and I was appointed as chief instructor. With my RAF training behind me this was no problem, but one of delight and satisfaction. I took the first Combined Services PTI advance course and then became a trade examiner for further courses. My adventure was growing day by day and year by year.

During this time I was playing much sport: basketball, squash, tennis and some rugby, although I did suffer a cartilage injury from playing rugby which affected me for some time. But with a good knowledge of rehabilitation, I soon recovered to continue playing to a high level, making the RNZAF basketball team and later the combined services team to play against Australia.

While working under my boss Flt. Lt.Peter Robertson, who was a geographer with an MSc degree from Canterbury University we set up the basis of survival training for aircrew. Peter piloted Catalinas during the war and was still currently flying so knew the important principles involved for survival.

This was exciting for me as I did not have good background knowledge of New Zealand conditions but was able to learn much from Peter Robertson. We did survival training for New Zealand conditions as well as open sea survival, Antarctic survival, and eventually jungle survival in Fiji. This type of training was given to all aircrew and eventually, we took all operational aircrew.

Jungle Survival Course in Fiji

The value of such training may have been criticised as unnecessary, but for us, it proved itself very valuable. Two of the pilots in the Antarctic Flight, Flt Lt. Jeffs and Flt. Lt Rule, crashed their Otter or Beaver aircraft during 'white out' conditions and remained with their crashed aircraft for ten days before being rescued. They attributed their confidence and survival to the training they had at Mount Cook under a glacial expert and mountaineer, Harry Ayres.

Harry Ayres was an expert on ice and snow at high altitudes and because of that was originally selected for the Everest expedition with Edmund Hillary. Hillary attributed much his success to the help and advice from Harry Ayres. For some controversial reason Harry was later excluded from the expedition because of the numbers involved.

The level of fitness of nearly all trainees was very high as shown by the physical rating tests we carried out with them. To go with this, the sporting success of teams from this Base in local and inter-base competitions was very high. During my time at this Base we won the inter-base basketball competition twice.

I was able to introduce for the first time in New Zealand a system of circuit training in which five or six exercises had to be done either in a time limit of one minute or to do as many as the person was able to do. These exercises included pull ups on a beam, astride jumps on to an off a bench holding a 5kg weight, rope climbs, sit ups on an inclined bench, barbell military press. Each person would first record their result and in successive training sessions would be required to do half of their maximum recorded, but twice during the training session. After several training sessions the they would retest themselves. This system proved popular because each person worked individually on their own level of fitness.

The ladder for me was reaching skyward each week but this was not all. I started to realise that if I wanted to achieve some of the goals I had, I needed to study and improve my educational deficiencies. So I enrolled through the Base educational officer to study for a Higher Educational Test, equal to a School Certificate and would serve to get me into higher education. I did pass an examination for an Associateship of the New Zealand Association of Health Physical Education and Recreation. More on this factor of education is given later in this book.

RAF School of PT Athletic team

I served at this Base for eight years and then was posted to an operational squadron, again being placed in charge of the PE & RT section. This was the sole charge position for me so I was only in charge of myself. Whilst there I marked the athletic track, looked after the swimming pool and the sports gear like cricket bats. We only had a small gymnasium and basketball court, but I had suggested optimistically that a new gymnasium and sports complex be built.

This was not to be for many years, but eventually, one was built. Was this going to be a pattern that would repeat itself for me? I had also suggested and planned for another Base to get a new gymnasium but did not get it until I had left the Base.

It was while at this Base that I completed my Higher Educational Test. Our sports teams were doing so well in inter base competitions with this Base winning the basketball, cricket and tennis competitions with the men's single champion coming from this Base for two years running. Individual fitness training was being done by many on the Base.

I was awarded a Gold Badge by the RNZAF Air Department for sporting participation, administration and coaching. This was a prestigious award and not given readily. The criteria for the award was frightening to read let alone do. This was awarded me during a routine parade.

After only two years I was posted to Woodbourne, in Blenheim in the South Island which was another major training Base. Again I was placed in charge with four instructors under me.

Posting to Woodbourne came with a promotion. I was promoted to Warrant Officer, the first PTI W/O since the war. This was a major training base for engine and airframe fitters and also a Boy Entrants School. I had a staff of four under me.

Apart from the training given to the trainees much of the work was to encourage greater personal fitness work and very active and successful sports' teams. I wrote a weekly sports bulletin which was included in the daily routine orders DROs which encourage many to get involved with their fitness.

One scheme that I promoted was to aim to swim 10 miles in March. I had about 30 take part. They would swim before work, during lunchtimes, and after work swimming any chosen number of lengths of the pool to complete the distance. Each day they would record with me the number of lengths they had done and I would publish progress reports in the weekly sports' bulletin.

The Boy Entrant School, each year held an outdoor training programme involving a confidence course set up in a wooded area, outdoor rifle range, and they were accommodated in small tents. I was visited one year by the Chief of Air Staff. He was most impressed with the quality of the training and thought it would be a good programme for many young people with social problems.

I was awarded a Chief of the Air
Staff Commendation in 1966 for my
'outstanding zeal and devotion to duty'

I retired from the RNZAF in 1968 to accompany my wife and two children back to England to visit our families, that were alive at that time but getting frail. I had tried to get an indulgence flight for my wife but there was no chance at that time and may not have been for a long time after I had applied.

There were regular flights to the UK by the

RNZAF but usually were filled by work-related needs such as the return of helicopter blades for replacement or repair. However, after I had farewelled my wife and two children I remained on the Base at Woodbourne and now had a billet in the Sergeants Mess quarters.

Just before the end of the year in 1968, I had a call to say I had been included on a C130 flight to the UK. This would get me to London on December 31, 1968, in time to meet my wife from the boat. A very happy and surprised wife and children met me at the boat terminal where they had arrived at. They had been away from me for the 6 weeks' journey and didn't know when I would be leaving New Zealand.

This it looked as if this part of my adventure was over, but was it? I had received so many favours and successes in New Zealand that it would have been tragic to have left those memories and many fine colleagues and friends in the RNZAF behind. I still held on to the possibility of returning, however, remote it was. But my goals had not been fulfilled so I just imagined them to be in the pending tray.

CHAPTER 5

Educational Achievements

For me with a deprived educational background in school because of the war situation, the challenge was to catch up on what I had missed and follow the hopes and goals that I established for myself. These lofty goals were very demanding but could be made possible by sustained motivation to reach the goal. They were stated earlier in this book - 'to become a doctor or a school teacher' Both these positions would require at least a matriculation to get me into a University or Training College.

I was now facing a very daunting challenge to keep working towards the gaols or giving up on them. But I didn't give up but worked one step at a time to gain a matriculation.

We were now in England having finished my twenty four years with both of the Air Forces and unable to get a teaching position until I had teaching certificate. This meant going to a College attached to a University.

This gave me another problem, 'how was I to pay for the training? I went to the local educational authority, LEA and applied and was told because I hadn't lived in England for the past 3 years I was not entitled to any grant. But I held on and applied for the grant which they gave me. This made my adventure even more challenging. But was this high adventure or not?

After three years at St Luke's College, University of Exeter I got a teaching position in a very good comprehensive school teaching science, biology, and mathematics and thought that this was the limit for me. But it wasn't. I knew that if I stayed in teaching I needed to become more qualified. My goal was still with me although I had reached one part of it as teacher. Now as a qualified teacher I made enquiries as to whether there were any vacancies back in New Zealand, because our two children that were born in New Zealand wanted to be back in their own country.

New Zealand House informed me there were, and invited me to London for an interview. I accepted their offer of a secondary school back in Blenheim where we had come from. Everything was fitting into this high adventure. The authorities paid our fares back to New Zealand, for the second time and I came to Marlborough College with a job and also a part of my goals as stated earlier in this book - it was to become a doctor or a school teacher. I was also given the position as manager of a coeducational hostel, something that I had no experience in. Both these new positions were a challenge, but where there is an adventure, there usually will be challenges to go with it.

I was allocated some difficult classes for my first year at the Marlborough Boys' College, many of them low stream students with little chance of gaining the standard School certificate, which was the secondary school GCSE, the general certificate of secondary education.

To go with this new challenge I enrolled for my first degree, a B.Ed.at Massey University in Palmerston North, NZ. Had I chosen too much with my limited background in schooling? So it was with apprehension that I started on the 21 papers required to gain the B.Ed in 1984.

Professor James Chapman and Professor Allan
Webster from Massey University NZ

In these early days computers were not the norm so I had either to write many assignments by pen and ink or to use a Brother typewriter which I had just purchased for the task. It was tedious and most of my assignments were complete after a busy day at school, not the freshest of minds, but the goal was there to spur me on. I did get some very pleasing grade results and eventually gained the B.Ed degree.

I had chosen educational papers that would help me to overcome some of the problems I was having with many of my low stream students. The systems that I tried only give small measure of success so I was determined to find what stopped a normal person from learning? Again the saying from Henry Ford was continually on my mind, 'If you think you can't or think that you can, you are right'. So if I could change their thinking I could change them, or more specifically if they could change their thinking, they would change. My adventure was growing day by day.

I introduced a practical science modular programme where the students would learn major science principles by making things such as a theodolite, microscope, or electric motors. This required many tools and basic skills of using them safely within a class room that would become noisy during the practical work involved. But the students liked what they are doing and the transfer of knowledge from one subject field to another was remarkable. For example having made an electric motor and remembered all the various names of parts such as commutator and armature, could be used during an English lesson to describe what they did, and also how they could prepare an advert for selling the motors.

This integration of subjects went on in several subject areas, English, Art, History etc. Now these low stream students were gradually becoming experts in a limited field but nevertheless experts from nothing. This was an increasing adventure for me and can be for anyone.

My studies were becoming enjoyable and productive in my teaching and therefore, I was looking forward to doing more advanced work during a Masters degree. But the awesomeness of such a bigger challenge required an increase motivation to pursue that step in the early stages.

However, my self confidence in my individuality type enabled me to carry on. My students were improving and behaviour problems were becoming less as my students were learning more.

To keep myself fit for the job I continued to play basketball for a teachers' team of 'Pedagogues' and to coach the College team, as well as play and coach tennis. I felt what I was doing was essential. Study, play and relaxation, and keep positive, and cheerful were essential features to have in such a busy life.

CHAPTER 6

Going Higher and Deeper

I started my M.Ed in 1994 at Massey University with six major papers to be completed including a dissertation on Individuality, learning problems, and disabilities, motivation, and gifted students. Each of these papers was challenging but leading me on to higher levels of understanding and adventure.

I particularly liked the years work on individuality for this was going to point me to major problems in learning; the problem associated with mismatch of learning style preference and teaching style. This led me to doing some research on achievement related to motivation and individuality type. It looked very promising that I had located an area contributing towards underachievement. If so, this could be a topic for the much higher degree of PhD. More on this later.

So, after twenty three years teaching I now felt that I had gained much more understanding to enable me to get good results and also to be able to pass on to other teachers and students. I gained very good result for my M.Ed(Hons) with an A+ for my dissertation but now at an age of 70. Was this too old to go on further?

Wife and Daughter at my Masters
degree. M.Ed (Hons) 1985

I had some amazing results from students who under the existing examination system where only 50% of all those sitting an exam in the country would pass, had little expectation from other teachers, their parents or themselves of being able to pass a school certificate exam. But gained an exceptional result with over 90% passing the exam. Such results convinced me of a number of things: one that it wasn't that low stream students couldn't learn but it was because they didn't want to learn because they could not see much value or purpose in what they were supposed to learn. They were unmotivated.

These years of experience showed me what was needed to overcome underachievement. Not that there was any magic in what I was wanting to do, although the results showed that it might be that, but the strategies had to be agreeable to each individuals' need. Therefore higher degree work was needed to give greater credibility to what I was wanting to do. But getting older, at 70, was it too late for such an adventure? Maybe not, why not try?

That was a question that I didn't want to answer or even consider, but was encouraged by my wife, Rita, to apply to do a PhD degree through Curtain University in Perth, Western Australia, which had been advertised in the local newspaper for students with a Master's degree in Education After all, Lord Tennyson wrote 'The Crossing of the Bar' at the age of 80, so although I was not Tennyson or 80 I did contact my eventual supervisor, Professor John Malone and told him about my success and he said that I was perfect material to pursue my doctorate by doing a thesis.

I could now picture the progress steps I was climbing towards Higher Adventure. It was not only challenging and beyond what I could think it was culminating towards a position of being able to help many others, particularly students.

The greater understanding I was getting from studies in Individuality types was pointing me towards a key to understanding how under achievement can occur. I found within my research that certain of the sixteen individual able to be identified by using a type inventory based upon a questionnaire were prone to fail at certain subjects. But did not have to fail if suitable intervention was made according to their type characteristics.

This was a major aid in identifying a common cause of underachievement. You may be wondering at this stage what is underachievement? I have defined at as 'failing to achieve what one has planned for, or what one can expect'.

Did this mean that there was to be some extensive planning to succeed or some high form of expectation?

I thought about this and asked many students what could they expect from an exam? Usually it was, 'to fail'. Now if I was to tell you that you will usually get what you expect would you be satisfied? Again they replied 'Is it as easy as that'. For a start it is, because your mind now wants to pass and your effort will start to improve to achieve what you expect. This together with strategies to show them their improvement was boosting their self esteem, one of those factors of motivation.

Getting to know more of their individuality features allowed me to use strategies that were agreeable to their personality type. Learning now became enjoyable both to them and for me. This is where my Masters' work on Myers- Briggs Type Inventory was paying off.

The other major subject studied in depth was motivation. So much is said about motivation but not completely understood. For there are different forms of motivation such as achievement motivation, and attributional motivation.

There is a relationship between them which will not be discussed here but later. It was something that I started to study in depth in 1947 when I was establishing my goals. I realised that there needed to be an inner force working to release energy to acquire what I had set my goals on. It was something that was within the brain centre that acted rather like a switch to turn off or on. When turned on energy flows to achieve what one sets their heart on. It can be influenced from without such as encouragement given by others such as teachers, parents of peers.

CHAPTER 7

Reaching the Mountain Top

I started my journey towards my PHD at Curtin University, Perth, Western Australia in 1999, just 70 years after being born. Sounds incredible but really it isn't. The title of my thesis was, **'The relationship Between Individual Type, Underachievement and the Attributional Motivation of Secondary School Science Students: Intervention Approaches for Underachievers'**

There have been many great accomplishments made by people even older than 80 such as Michelangio and Lord Tennyson. But for me the journey had begun. 'Now this is where the rubber hits the road' or that is what it felt like. This surely was an answer to a 'What's Next?' question from the newspaper reporter when reporting on my achievement with a PhD and to publish a book at 87. And now even publishing another book at 90 and 91. Does it ever stop?

I now had enough background in underachievement

after an equivalent 40 years of experience with students from my earlier studies, I felt I had a good grasp to take this on even further. I wanted to find out if there was any significant relationship between individual type and underachieving at science, which was the subject I was teaching. There certainly were some types found to be significantly related to underachievement. This did not mean that those types were doomed to underachieve, but were likely to unless some intervention strategy was employed to prevent it.

Intervention strategies were included within my thesis so that not only was a problem identified, and causes found but also what could be done to prevent or overcome any underachievement during my teaching.

I was aware that there could be other reasons beyond my help that could be causing learning problems and therefore, I wanted to locate and identify among a group of senior students that were underachieving, any of these problems and be able to rectify them with the classroom activities.

This latter point was important because that was what was needed to be worked on to change the situation for the students. I would not be able to change the home situation or conditions of the student, or the government, but I could change the teaching strategies to accommodated differences in individuality.

My research started with identifying the individual types of senior students who are underachieving or who had previously achieved but had dropped off. Then I would identify their type and statistically test to see if there was any significance with my findings. There surely was, as I could have expected, because of the the range of types within my research population.

Following the type analysis I interviewed each student to find out their views and importance of motivation. They all agreed that it was important but did not know how to increase it or improve it. Most thought that it came extrinsically from outside influences. They were not wrong but only partly right.

The relationship between achievement motivation and attributional motivation is a vital factor to increase overall motivation for each student, or for anyone wanting to achieve greater things by improving their motivation. I had practiced this technique on myself over the years and found it very effective. Why?

The answer to the above question is the clue to improve achievement. Words are very effective tools and has the effect upon one's thinking, and it is thinking that changes ones attitude from failure to success, from can't to can as, Henry Ford said. Such attributional words as, 'With the right strategy I can solve this problem'. 'It is getting easier as I work on it'. These attributions will now start to change ones achievement motivation or attitude towards what the student may be learning. The better the attitude a learner has, the better the results will be. It is not just a case of mind over matter but 'where the mind goes, the man follows.

Dr. Len and wife Rita at his graduation

CHAPTER 8

Other Books by this Author

This author's has written several self-improvement books suitable for students, teachers and parents. Both of them are based upon the authors 40 years as a Teacher within secondary schools in England and New Zealand, also 24 years in the RAF and RNZAF as a Physical Fitness instructor.

He has a B.Ed, M.Ed(Hons) PhD, and a TTC (Trained Teaching Certificate)

'In Pursuit of Success Overcoming Underachievement,'

This book contains an individuality questionnaire to determine your personality or individually type based upon the Myers-Briggs Type Inventory. A description of the characteristics of each of the 16 individuality types.

Contains a list of jobs with various levels of probability for success for each type.

Good analysis of various forms of motivation.

A Goal setting chart.

Issues relating to Underachievement.

Example of a Mind-map for improving memory and for quick revision recall.

The following is the press release for this book.

A companion to "In Pursuit of Success: Overcoming Underachievement," this book answers a question commonly asked regarding achievement or failure, or one of surprise. It encourages people to move from where they are at as far as achievements go and determine where they would like to go.

"Based upon my research and personal experience, it is possible to advance from where one may be to where one may want to be," Restall says. "A very good strategy to help you to deal with what is next is to look outward at what is involved, look inward to what gifts you have, look upward for inspiration and look forward to what results you are expecting."

"What's Next?"

This book asks the question of you or for you to ask yourself the question after having failed or succeeded at something. Or it may just be a surprise exclamation after some event. It covers ways of answering the question.

It aims to remind readers that life is a continuing journey with exciting prospects on the way and one's success should be the stepping-stone to another one. "This book gives positive steps to advance from any expression of 'What's next?' and enables you to find yourself achieving great success. Avoid the tendency to stay where you are but go where you would like to be.

CHAPTER 9

End of this Phase of High Adventure

This story is rather like a classic story where the hero wins the prize or the fair maiden, and then they live happily ever after together. I certainly did win the prize and marry the lovely Rita, and reach all the goals, and lived happily ever after until my beloved died in 2015. It was largely through the encouragement and support from my wife Rita that enabled my adventure to succeed.

I had set goals back in1947 but not quite understanding them at that time caused them to be stalled from to time. I since had learned that goals need to be set and kept in focus to cause them to come to pass.

For every adventure embarked upon will be accompanied with a challenge. The bigger the adventure, the bigger the challenge and it is this that stops many people from taking on big adventures unless they have big means of overcoming the challenges. For instance, finance may be involved that seems beyond the adventurer. Ask yourself the question, 'What's Next?' to give you a good reason to take on a challenge.

I had wanted to take another PhD because I had found out so much with my first that I wanted to go beyond that. But the finance required from me as pensioner were out of the question. I had made a personal decision not to 'owe no man anything' so would not go into debt. I had been fortunate for my first PhD to have been given it free of all charges and fees.

As my story unfolds from a young boy leaving school with no qualifications it looked as if the goals that I was setting were beyond me. I suppose they were at the time of making them, but I had come to recognise the value of motivation to release internal energy, not without effort, to accomplish the goals set back in 1947

This book has highlighted my exciting adventures

and for those that were in support of what I was doing. Adventure occurs for us all at various stages in our lives and it is what we do with the adventure that really matters. In my case, every small thing I attempted became an adventure and one small success would lead me on to bigger ones. I hadn't realised until I started to write these events down that I was always searching for success. What is shown by this story or account of my thrilling life is that I gained success in most activities I was engaged in, with sport or education and in my love with my wife Rita.

The book, 'What's Next?' a companion to "In Pursuit of Success: Overcoming Underachievement," answers a question commonly asked regarding achievement or failure, or one of surprise. It encourages people to move from where they are at as far as achievements go and determine where they would like to go.

Based upon my research and personal experience, it

is possible to advance from where one may be to where one may want to be. A very good strategy to help you to deal with what is next is to look outward at what is involved, look inward to what gifts you have, look upward for inspiration and look forward to what results you are expecting.

You may have noticed that my adventures really started when I established those goals back in1947 so this may give you a clue as to how your adventures may begin.

As you read this you may be thinking about some adventures you may want to embark on. Well, they can be rather like goals. They don't need to be grandiose ones like wanting to save the world, although for some people that could be a worthwhile goal for them. I think of that young girl addressing the United Nations in New York regarding climate change. Her goal was to convict and convince the delegates that they needed to do more to save the planet. Her goal was strong enough for her to pursue that goal with much success and she became the person of the year.

Write your goals down and give them the priority of importance. Hold on to them and see them being fulfilled one by one.

"We have all been placed on this earth to discover our own path, and we will never be happy if we live someone else's idea of life."

James Van Praagh

Lightning Source UK Ltd.
Milton Keynes UK
UKHW041825030820
367650UK00002B/36/J

9 781543 496260